Texts from

Bruce Codex.

This codex of Coptic, Arabic and Ethiopic manuscripts was found in upper Egypt by a Scottish traveler, James Bruce in about 1769. The first translations of the text began to be made in the mid-1800's.

The passages below are based on the 1892 translation of

Carl Schmidt.

The Bruce Codex

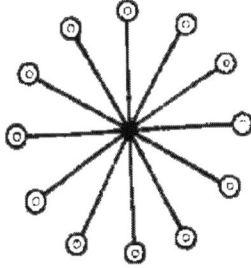

Archive Notes on The Bruce Codex:

I. The First Book of Ieou

II. The Untitled Text

III. An Unnamed Gnostic Hymn from the Bruce Codex

IV. An Unnamed Gnostic Text from the Bruce Codex

History of the Bruce Codex

This codex, which comprises Coptic. Arabic and Ethiopic manuscripts, is said to have been bought at Medinet Habu in Upper Egypt in about 1769 by the Scottish traveller. James Bruce.' We owe this information to C. G. Woide who made the first copy of the Coptic gnostic texts contained in it. He also first brought them to public notice with an article on the Egyptian version of the Bible, and he gave the biblical citations in his *Appendix ad editionem Novi Testamenti*. After his death his copy of the texts was held by the Clarendon Press, Oxford, under the number MS. Clarendon Press d. 13. In 1848 the codex was acquired by the Bodleian Library, together with Woide's transcript of the gnostic texts. The gnostic manuscripts were catalogued under the number Bruce 96.

M. G. Schwartze was the next to transcribe these texts when he was in England in 1848. On comparing Woide's copy with the originals, he found a number of mistakes, but his death unfortunately occurred before his work was completed. His amended copy became the property of H. Petermann, at whose death the copy finally came into the hands of A. Erman.

In the meantime in 1882 E. Amelineau began to work on the text. Two preliminary communications appeared in 1882 and 1887, and in 1890 an introduction to his translation of the text (Bibl. 2). The latter was published in 1891 (Bibl. 3).

In 1890 Erman and Hanack were instrumental in arranging that Schmidt should work on the manuscript in Oxford, with the support of the Akademie der Wissenschaften of Berlin. With the help of the copies made by Woide and Schwartze, Schmidt was able to distinguish that there were two manuscripts and some fragments in the one codex. He put the leaves in sequence and made a new transcript of the texts. Schmidt's page order was later followed by the Bodleian authorities when. in 1928, they renumbered the leaves. Schmidt published his edition of the text with a German translation and commentary in 1892 (Bibl. 32). No further editions of the whole text have appeared. In 1905 Schmidt published a revised translation (Bibl. 35). The volume contained translations of the Pistis Sophia as well as the texts of the Bruce Codex, together with commentaries on both codices. Two new editions by Till of this volume have subsequently appeared (see p. 321).

In 1918 an English translation of the manuscript known as the Untitled Text was published by F. Lamplugh (Bibl. 23) This was based on Amelineau's French version.

A transcript and English translation of the Untitled Text was made by C. A. Baynes in 1933 (Bibl, 9). She based her work on the original manuscript, using the published transcript by Schmidt and the copies of Woide and Schwartze for comparison. Her arrangement of the leaves differed from that of Schmidt, in that she placed his five final leaves at the beginning, The Untitled Text was photographed at this time, and photographic reproductions of the leaves were included in this edition of the text. The other manuscript was photographed later.

Description of the Manuscript

The Bruce Codex originally consisted of 78 papyrus leaves (156 pages) of which seven leaves - in existence when Woide made his copy - are now missing. Each page, with the exception of two, is inscribed in one column, on both recto and verso, There are from 27 to 34 lines to a page. Woide noted that the condition of the papyrus was poor, and in the course of a century the subsequent deterioration of the manuscript, as recorded by Schmidt, Baynes and Till, has been considerable.

When acquired the codex consisted of loose leaves, the original order of which had been lost, One leaf alone carried numbers, and Woide was only able to make a page-by-pm transcript without distinguishing the documents. In 1886 the authorities of the Bodleian Library caused the loose leaves of the codex to be bound in book form. The leaves were bound without regard to order or sequence. Many were placed upside-down and with the recto and verso reversed Each leaf, wax enclosed between two sheets of tracing paper.

It is due to the work of Schmidt that the codex now stands in its present form. The codex consists of two independent manu- scripts and some fragments. The first manuscript, to which Schmidt gave the title "The First and Second Books of Jeu, comprised 47 leaves (94 pages) of which three leaves were missing. The second, called the "Untitled Text", contained 31 leaves (62 pages, of which four were missing. Schmidt included the fragments (8 leaves) with the first manuscript.

Each of the two main texts is written in a different hand, and the two manuscripts bear no obvious relation to one another. The first is written in a cursive hand on papyrus of a pale colour. The second is in an uncial script on a darker and more reddish papyrus. Not only are the first and second manuscripts the work of different scribes, but the fragments are in handwriting which differs again from these. At the beginning of the first document Schmidt has placed a frontispiece consisting of a leaf bearing a cross in the form of an ankh sign. Greek monograms occur in relation to the arms of the cross.' The Books of Jeu contain a number of cryptograms and gnostic diagrams. A leaf with a border is placed by Schmidt at the end of the Books of Jeu; this contain the two fragments noted above.

The manuscript, re-bound and with its leaves renumbered, is now unfortunately in very poor condition. The papyrus of many leaves is defective and there are opaque dark spots due to previous mildew. Details of the condition of individual leaves are given in the footnotes on the Coptic text. The writing is so faded as to be almost illegible, even when viewed with ultra-violet light.

The title by which the first two texts are generally known does not appear in the Bruce Codex. It is derived from a reference to the "two Books of Jeu" in the Pistis Sophia text. The contents of the present texts suggested to Schmidt and others that these treatises were the "Books of Jeu", and originated from a milieu similar to that of the Pistis Sophia. In only one text, the first, is the title preserved; this stands at the end and reads "The Book of the great Logos corresponding to Mysteries".

There are two incomplete copies of the opening pages of the First Book of Jeu. The first copy, after some initial words, runs from page 1 of the manuscript to the foot of page 4 where the text breaks off (Schmidt 39.1-44.5). The second copy with the same initial words begins on page 1a and ends on page 4a (Schmidt 44.6-47.7). After a lacuna, the text begins again on page 5 and reads consecutively to the foot of page 34 (Schmidt 47.9-78.23). Pages 8-34 contain a series of diagrams bearing names of Jeu and numbered from 1 to 28, the 13th being omitted. There is no indication as to whether the series is complete. After a lacuna the text begins again on page 35 (Schmidt 79.7) with the fifth stanza of a gnostic hymn, of which the first four stanzas are missing. The hymn appears to end at the foot of page 38 (Schmidt 82.26). After a lacuna the text begins again on page 39 (Schmidt 83.5) and runs consecutively to the foot of page 53 where it concludes with the title (Schmidt 99.5).

The text of the Second Book of Jeu begins on page 54 (Schmidt 99.6) and runs consecutively to the foot of page 86 (Schmidt 138.4). The end of the text is missing. On the single leaf which follows, page 87 contains a fragment of a gnostic hymn (Schmidt 139.1-140.14), and on page 88 is a description of the passage of the soul (Schmidt 140.15-141.21).

The Untitled Text lacks both beginning and end. According to the pagination of Schmidt, the text runs consecutively from pages 1 to 51 (Schmidt 226.1-264.6). Pages 52-61 are five leaves of uncertain relation to the rest of the text, which Schmidt places at the end (Schmidt 264.9-277.8). In her edition of the text (Bibl. 9) Baynes places these leaves at the beginning, but for the reasons given below the page order of Schmidt and Till has been retained here.

Both texts of the Bruce Codex appear to be compilations, and similar or related "documents" are either grouped together or placed one following another in sequence. Occasionally the present chapter divisions may indicate where one document ends and another begins. This method of composition gives rise to repetitions in the narrative, and to a lack of overall continuity. Thus in the Books of Jeu, Chapters 49-52 appear to be variant accounts of what has already then given in Chapters 42ff. In the Untitled Text, Chapters 6 and 10 may be different descriptions of the same phenomena. As the unplaced leaves forming Chapter 21 contain material similar to that in Chapters 1, 2, 7, and 17. and are perhaps part of a separate version of the whole text, it seems appropriate to piece them at the end of the treatise.

A brief summary of the contents of the Books of Jeu and the Untitled Text a given here for the convenience of the reader. An attempt has been made to indicate the most outstanding motifs in each chapter, but in many cases the selection is necessarily a rather arbitrary one.

Contents

II

emanations which were emanated when the Father moved Jeu).

(Lacuna)

Fragment of a gnostic hymn: a hymn of praise to the First Mystery who caused Jeu to establish the 12 aeons, the 24 emanations etc.

33-38 Teaching by Jesus to his disciples concerning the treasuries (the beginning is missing; only the 56th-60th treasuries remain); the procedures for entering them; diagrams representing their seals of which the names are given; the names to be spoken while holding ciphers in the hand; the drawing bank of the watchers, the ranks and the veils so that the gate into the treasury can be crossed.

39 Inquiry by the disciples why all these places, fatherhoods and they themselves have come into existence; another account by Jesus of the small idea which his Father did not withdraw to himself; the emanating from it of Jesus as first emanation; the three voices given forth from the idea which became all the places; the emanation of the 12 emanations.

Instructions by Jesus to the disciples that they are a rank, that they will proceed with Jesus in all the places, and that will call them disciples.

40 Request by the disciples to be told the name which suffices for all the places in the treasuries, so that they are drawn back; reply by Jesus that he will say it to them.

Inquiry by the disciples whether it is the name of the Father of Jesus; reply by Christ that it is not, but that when the name of the great power is said, all the places, ranks, veils and watchers arc drawn hack. Teaching (by Jesus) of the procedure for invoking the great name, the diagram, seal and cipher. so that the disciples pass to the place of the true God which is outside the places of his Father; warning that the name should not be said continually.

41 Hymn of praise spoken by Jesus who, with his disciples, had proceeded inwards to the 7th treasury; glorifications of his Father, each ending with the question "What now, O unapproachable God?". to which the disciples respond "Amen, amen, amen" three times.

(The title "The great Logos corresponding to Mysteries" is given after the end of the hymn).

The Books of Jeu Book 2

Chapter 42 Teaching by Jesus to his disciples and women disciples on the mysteries of the Treasury of the Light, which after death erase the sins of the soul, and enable it to pass through all the places of the invisible God until it reaches the Treasury of the Light.

43 Warning to the disciples not to give these mysteries to any but those worthy of them, or in exchange for any goods of this world: especially are they not to be given to those who serve the 72 archons or the 8 powers of the great archon, the third power of which is Taricheas, son of

Sabaoth, the Adamas; they are only to be given to those who are as the Sons of the Light.

Promise by Jesus to his disciples to give to them the mysteries, but first the three baptisms and the mystery of taking away the evil of the archons, afterwards the spiritual injunction: instructions to those receiving these mysteries.

44 Reproach by the disciples that Jesus had not told them the mysteries of the Treasuries of the Light promise by Jesus to give them the mysteries of all the places of the Treasury of the Light, and that he who performs them needs no other mystery except the mystery of the forgiveness of sins; that those who have received all these will pass through all places to the place of Jeu; promise by Jesus to fulfil the disciples in every mysteries so that they might be called "Sons of the Pleroma".

45 Instructions by Jesus for performing the baptism of water: ritual offering by Jesus of wine and bread in the presence of the disciples; sealing of the disciples with a seal.

Prayer-invocation by Jesus to his Father that the 15 helpers who serve the 7 virgins of the light come and baptise the disciples in the water of life; invocation to Zorokothora to bring forth water in one of the pitchers of wine as a sign: transformation of the wine into water, and baptism of the disciples by Jesus, giving them from the offering and sealing them with a seal; rejoicing of the disciples over their baptism.

46 Instructions by Jesus for performing the baptism of fire: ritual offering of wine and bread with incense; sealing of the disciples with a seal.

Prayer-invocation by Jesus to his Father that Zorokothora Melchisedek come and bring the water of the baptism of fire of the Virgin of the Light, that the Virgin of the Light baptise the disciples and purify them: appearance of a sign in the fire of the incense, and baptism of the disciples, giving them from the offering and sealing them with a seal; rejoicing of the disciples over their baptism.

47 Instructions by Jesus for performing the baptism of the Holy Spirit ritual offering of wine and bread with incense, sealing of the disciples with a seal. Prayer-invocation by Jesus to his Father. calling upon the names of the Treasury of the Light; appearance of a sign in the offering, and baptism of the disciples, giving them from the offering and sealing them with a seal, rejoicing of the disciples over their baptism.

48 Ritual offering by Jesus of the incense of the mystery for taking away the evil of the archons, sealing of the disciples with a seal.

Prayer-invocation by Jesus to his Father that Adamas and his rulers come and take away the evil from the disciples; sealing of the disciples with a seal, and the ceasing of evil in them, rejoicing of the disciples.

49 Another account of a promise by Jesus to give to the disciples the "defenses" of all the places, with their baptisms, offerings, seals, ciphers and names, and the manner of invoking them in order to pass within them. Instructions to the disciples on the coming forth of their souls; promise of entry into the Treasury of the Light. and withdrawal of all the aeons and of the watchers if the disciples have received the mystery of the forgiveness of sins.

50 Another account of a promise (by Jesus) to the disciples about the passage of their souls through the ranks. in each of which they would be given the seal, mystery and name of that rank and pass to its interior, finally reaching Jeu, the father of the Treasury of the Light. Another account of the innermost rank as 12th rank of the 12th great power of the emanations of the true God; prayer-invocation to the true God to send a light-power to the 12 disciples, they having received the mystery of the forgiveness of sins.

Another account of a promise to give to the disciples this mystery with its de fences and its seal.

51 Teaching by Jesus that to he Sons of the Light it is necessary to receive the mystery of the forgiveness of sins: request by the disciples to be given this mystery.

52 Another account of teaching by Jesus to his disciples concerning the coming forth of their soul: de fences to be given at each of the 12 aeons in order to proceed upwards; diagrams representing seals of which the names are given: the names to he spoken while holding a cipher in the hand; sealing and prayer-invocation calling upon the archons to withdraw.

Defences to be given at the 13th aeon to the 24 emanations of the invisible God: diagram representing the seal of which the names arc given; prayer-invocation calling upon the 24 emanations to withdraw.

A similar procedure at the 14th aeon where is the second invisible God with three archons of the light; teaching on the impossibility of further progress into the Treasury of the Light without having received the mystery of the forgiveness of sins; seal and cipher, and the prayer-invocation to be spoken.

(The end is missing)

Fragment of a gnostic hymn.

Fragment on the passage of the soul through the archons of the way of the midst.

The Untitled Text

Chapter 1 The city; the First Father of the All; the self-originated place: the deep; silence: the first space; the first sound.

2 Coming into existence of the second place called demiurge, logos, understanding (mind), man; the column. the overseer; the Father of the All; the Cross; the monad; the ennead. the 12 deeps; the image of the Father; the incorporeal members out of which Man came into existence.

3 The Father, the second demiurge; the forethought, the creator of the pleroma; the 4 gates, 4 monads, 24 helpers, 24 myriad powers; the overseer. the Setheus; Aphrêdon and his 12 beneficent ones; Adam of the light and his 365 aeons: the rule; the Child; the thought which comes forth from the deep.

4 The deep (containing) 3 fatherhood, the first, the covered one; the second (containing) the table, the logos: the third (containing) the silence, the source, the 12 beneficent ones, the 5 seals. the all-mother; the ennead which completes a decad from the monad.

5 The immeasurable deep (containing) the table; the 3 greatnesses; the sonship called Christ, the Verifier, who seals each one with the seal of the Father; his 12 aspects; the 12 sources; the 12 spaces which produce the Christ. the Fruit of the All.

6 The deep of Setheus; the 12 Fatherhoods surrounding him, each with 3 aspects, making 36 in number; the 12 surrounding his head; the diagram.

7 Man as kinsman of the mysteries; witness of Marsanes and Nicotheus; revelation concerning the triple-powered perfect one.

The only-begotten one hidden in the Setheus; the 12 fatherhoods in the type of the 12 apostles, each making 365 powers in his right hand; the 30 powers in his left hand; the Only One from whom the monad containing all things came; the city or man, crowned by monads; the mother-city of the only-begotten one, of whom Phosilampes spoke; the monad which is in the Setheus like a concept; the creative word, the creative mind, to whom the creation prays as God; blessing from the All to the only-begotten one.

8 The light-spark sent by Setheus to the indivisible pleroma; the man of light and truth; the servant of the pleroma; sending of the light-spark to the matter below. sending of Gamaliel, Strempsuchos and Agramas as watchers and helpers to those who received the light-spark.

9 The 12 springs and 12 fatherhoods in the place of the indivisible one; the crown in which is every species of life; the crown in which are 365 species, from which all the aeons receive crowns; the god-bearing land in the midst of the indivisible one; the all-mother; the rule in the midst of the all-mother; the only-begotten one to whom blessing is given; receiving of Christhood by the only-begotten one.

10 Another account of the rule which is within each of 9 enneads in which are 3 fatherhoods; the imperishable place called the holy land; the immeasurable deep with 12 fatherhoods above it, 30 powers surrounding each; 365 fatherhoods by which the year was divided; Musanios and Aphrêdon with his 12 beneficent ones; prayers of the mother of all things.

Agitation of the pleroma; drawing back of the veils, re-establishment of the aeons by the overseer; coming forth of the triple-powered one in whom the son was hidden; sending forth by Setheus of the creative word which became Christ.

12 Giving of rank to her worlds by the mother; laying therein of the light-spark; placing of the forefather and 12 beneficent ones, with their crowns, a seal and a source; a rule with 12 fathers and a sonship.

Setting up of the progenitor son in the type of the triple-powered one; making of a world, an aeon and a city; the god-bearing earth; the crown sent by the Father to the progenitor son; the garment sent by the first monad; the veil.

13 Separation of the existent from the non-existent, as "eternal" and "matter"; placing of veils between them: giving of 10 aeons to the mother; giving of the rule with 3 powers, 12 powers and 7 powers to her; setting up of the forefather in the aeons of the mother of all things; giving of powers and glories to the forefather; giving of a sonship and of a power from the aeon called Solmistos to him.

14 Creation of an aeon by the forefather, according to the command of the Father hidden in the silence; wish of the forefather to turn the All to the hidden Father; prayer of the mother to the thrice-begotten one.

15 Setting up of the eternal self-father by the mother; giving of the mystery of the hidden Father to those who fled to the aeon of the self-father; knowledge of the mystery which became Man.

16 Establishment by the mother of her first-born son; her gift to him of a garment containing all bodies; dividing of all matter into species by the progenitor; his giving of law to the species; his bringing them forth from the darkness of matter.

17 Song of praise by the mother of the All to the infinite and unknowable One. who begot Man in his mind; to him who gave all things to Man who wrapped himself in the creation like a garment; prayer of the mother that he give ranks to her offspring; her wish that her offspring should know the changeless One as Saviour.

18 Coming of the light-spark from the infinite one; wonder of the aeons as to where he had been hidden before he revealed himself; song of praise by the powers of the pleroma who saw him; making of a veil for their worlds.

19 Separation of matter into two lands. on the right and on the left, by the Lord of the whole earth; setting of boundaries and veils between them; giving of laws and commandments to those on the right; promise of eternal life. of the knowledge that God is within them, and that they are as gods.

20 Prayer of those begotten of matter that incorporeal spirits be sent to teach them; sending of powers of discernment; establishment of ranks according to the hidden ordinance.

Immersion in the name of the self-begotten one; the source of living water: Michar and Micheu, the powers which are over it; Barpharanges and the Pistis Sophia; Sellao, Eleinos, Zogenethles, Selmelche; the 4 lights : Eleleth, Daveide, Oroiael,

(Lacuna)

21 Account of the Father of the All; his insubstantial members; the son; the city or man portraying the All: likeness of the body of Man to the aeons of the pleroma ; the God-man whom the All desires to know; hymn of blessing and praise to him.

The First Book of IEOU

I have loved you. I have wanted life to be given you; the Living Jesus, who knows the truth.

Chapter 1

This is the book of the gnoses of the invisible God, by
means of the hidden mysteries which show the way to the
chosen race, leading in refreshment to the life of the Father
- in the coming of the Saviour , of the deliverer of souls who
receive themselves the Word of life which is higher than all
life - in the knowledge of the living Jesus, who has come
forth through the Father from the aeon of light at the
completion of the Pleroma - in the teaching, apart from
which there is no other, which the living Jesus has thaught
to his apostles, saying: "This is the teaching in which dwells
the whole knowledge." The living Jesus answered and said
to his disciples: "Blessed is he who has crucified the world,
and who has not the world to crucify him." The apostles
answered with one voice, saying : "O Lord, teach us the
way to crucify the world, that it may not crucify us, so that
we are destroyed and loose our lives" The living Jesus
answerd : "He who has crucified it is he who has found my
word and has fulfilled it according to the will of him who
has sent me."

Chapter 2

The apostles answered, saying : " Speak to us, O Lord, that
we may hear thee. We have followed thee with our whole
hearts. We have left behind father and mother, we have left
behind vineyards and fields, we have left behind goods and
the greatness of kings, and we have followed thee, so that
thou shouldst teach us to know the life of thy father who
has sent thee" The living Jesus answered and said : "The life
of my Father is this : that you receive your soul from the
race of understanding mind, and that it ceases to be earthly
and becomes understanding through that which I say to you
in the course of my discourse, so that you fulfil it and are
saved from the archon of this aeon and his persecutions, to
which there is no end. But you, my disciples, hasten to
receive my word with certaintiy so that you know it, in
order that the archon of this aeon may not fight with you -
this one who did not find any commandment of his in me -
so that you also, my apostles, fulfil my word in relation to
me, and I myself make you free, and you become whole
through a freedom in which there is no blemish. As the
Spirit of the comforter (Parakleiton) is whole, so will you
also be whole, through the freedom of the spirit of the Holy
Comforter."

Chapter 3

All the apostles, Matthew and John, Philip and
Bartholomew and James, answered with one voice, saying:

"O Lord Jesus, thou who livest, whose goodness extends
over those who have found thy wisdom and thy form in
which thou gavest light ; O light-giving Light that
enlightened our hearts until we received the light of life; O
true Word, that through gnosis teaches us the hidden
knowledge of the Lord Jesus, the living one."

The living Jesus answered and said : "Blessed is the man
who has known these things. He has brought heaven down,
he has lifted the earth and has sent it to heaven, and he has
become the Midst for it is nothing." The apostles answered,
saying : "Jesus , thou living one, Lord , interprete for us
how we may bring heaven down, for we have followed thee
in order that thou shouldst teach us the true light." The
living Jesus answered and said : "The Word which existed in
heaven before the earth came into existence - this which is
called the world - but you, when you know my Word, you
will bring heaven down, and it will dwell in you. Heaven is
the invisible Word of the Father; but when you know these
things you will bring heaven down. As to sending the earth
up to heaven, I will show you what it is , that you may know
it : to send the earth to heaven is that he who hears the
word of gnosis has ceasedto have the understanding mind
of man of earth, but has become a man of heaven. His
understanding mind has ceased to be earthly, but it has

become heavenly. Because of this you will be saved from the archon of this aeon, and he will become the Midst, because it is nothing." The living Jesus said again : "When you become heavenly you will become the Midst because it is nothing, for the .. . .. rulers and the wicked powers (exousiai) will you and they will envy you because you have known me, because I am not from the world, and I do not resemble the rulers and the powers (exousiai) and all the wicked ones. They do not come from me. And furthermore he who (is born) in the flesh of unrighteousness has no part in the Kingdom of my Father, and also he who me according to the flesh has no hope Kingdom of God the Father."

Chapter 4

The Apostles answered with one voice, they said : "Jesus , ,
O Lord, are we born of the flesh, and known thee according
to the flesh? Tell us, O Lord, for we are troubled." The
living Jesus answered and said to his apostles : " I do not
speak of the flesh in which you dwell, but the flesh of and
non-understanding which exists in ignorance, which leads
astray many from the of my Father." The apostles answered
the words of the living Jesus, the said: "Tell us how non-
understanding happens, that we may beware of it, lest we
should go . . . ." The living Jesus answered and said : "
one who bears my virginity and my . . . . . and my garment,
without understanding and knowing me, and blasphemes
my name, I have . . . . to destruction. And furthermorse he
has become an earthly son because he has not known my
word with certainity - these which the Father spoke, so that
I myself should teach those who will know me at the
completion of the pleroma of him who sent me." The
Apostles answered and said : "O Lord Jesus, thou living
one, teach us the completion, and it suffices us." And he
said : "The word which I give to you yourselves...."

Chapter 5

He has emanated ' him, being of this type ... This is the true God. He will set him up in this type as head'. He will be called Jeu '. Afterwards my Father will move him to bring forth other emanations, so that they fill these places. This is his name according to the treasuries 4 which are outside this. He will be called by this name: ..., that is to say: 'The true God' '. He will set him up in this type as head over the treasuries' which are outside this. This is the type of the treasuries over which he will set him as head, and this is the manner in which the treasuries are distributed, he being their head. This is the type in which he was before he was moved to bring forth emanations:

Jeu, the true God	....This is his type
This is his name ...	This now is the form in which....

	....(has emanated). This is his name. He will be called the true God

Furthermore he will be called Jeu. He will be father of a multitude of emanations. And a multitude of emanations will come forth from him through the command of my Father, and they themselves will be fathers of the treasuries. I will place a multitude as heads over them, and they will be called Jeu, the true God. It is he who will be father of all the Jeus, because he is an emanation of my Father. And the true God will emanate through the command of my Father. He will be head over them. He will move them ' and a multitude of emanations will come forth from all the Jeus, through the command of my Father when he moves them, and they will fill all the treasuries. And they will be called ranks of the Treasuries of the Light. Myriads upon myriads will come into existence from them. This now is the type in which the true. God is placed when he is about to be set up as head over the treasuries, before he has brought forth emanations over the treasuries, and before he has brought forth emanations, because my Father has not yet moved him to bring forth and to set up. This is his type which I have already set forth, but this is his type when he will bring forth emanations. This is the type of the true God in the manner in which he is placed:

The three lines which are thus, they are the voices which he
will give out when he is commanded to sing praises to the
Father, so that he himself brings forth emanations, and he
also emanates This is the type of what he is:

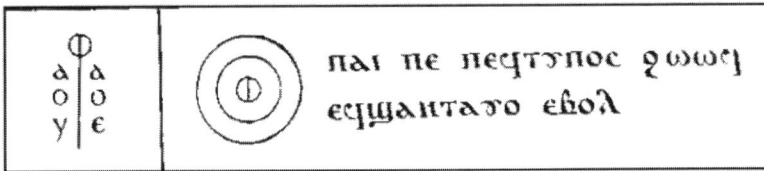

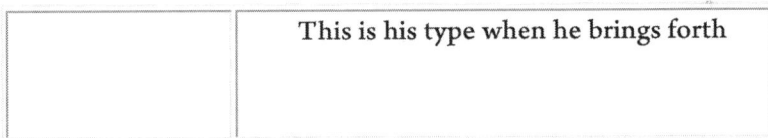

а а о о у є		ⲡⲁⲓ ⲡⲉ ⲡⲉϥⲧⲩⲡⲟⲥ ϩⲱⲱϥ ⲉϥϣⲁⲛⲧⲁⲩⲟ ⲉⲃⲟⲗ

	This is his type when he brings forth

This moreover is the manner in which the true God is
placed as he is about to emanate emanations, when he is
moved by m Father to bring forth emanations, and to set
them up as head over the treasuries, through the command
of my Father '. A multitude come forth from them and they

31

fill all the treasuries through the command of my Father, in order to become god(s). The true God will be called Jeu, the father of all the Jeus; his name in the tongue of my Father is this: ... But when he is set up as head over all the treasuries, in order to emanate them, this now is his type which I have finished setting forth.

Chapter 6

Hear now also the type of the treasuries how they are
emanated; he will become head over them in this way,
before he has emanated them; this is his type, as he is
placed. Now the true God was of this type.

ⲡⲁⲓ   ⲅⲱϥ ⲟⲛ ⲡⲉ (ⲡⲉ)ϥⲭⲁ=
ⲣⲁⲕⲧⲏⲣ ⲉϥϩⲓ-ⲡⲉϥϩⲟ ⲛⲧⲉⲓϩⲉ

This is his character which is on his face thus

But I have called upon the name of my Father, so that he should move the true God in order to emanate. But he himself caused This is his character ' an idea (thought) to come forth which is on his face thus: from his treasuries.

A power of my Father moved the true God. It radiated within him through this small idea (thought) ' which came forth from the treasuries of my Father. It radiated within the true God. A mystery moved him through my Father. The true God gave voice, saying thus: ... And when he had given voice, there came forth this voice which is the emanation. It was of this type as it proceeded forth from one side after another of each treasury. The first voice is this, which Jeu, the true God, called, which came forth from him, the one above.

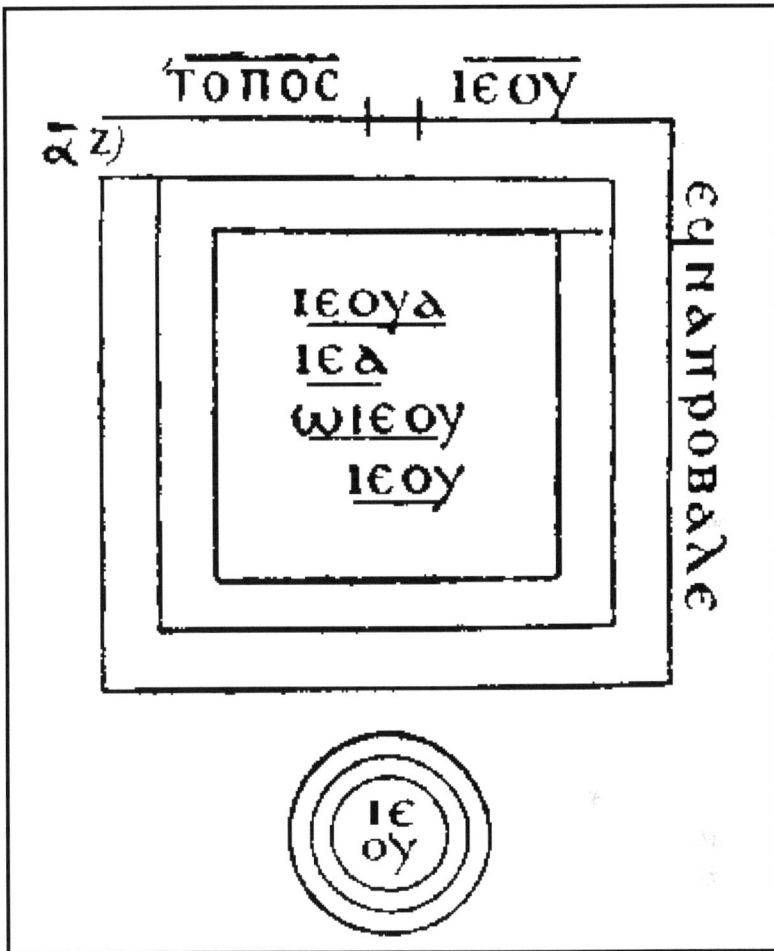

(Jeu1) .... Place .... Jeu

He will emanate

... ... Jeu

... ... Jeu

This is his character. He will set up a rank corresponding to the treasuries,
and will place it as watchers' at the gate' of the treasuries which are those
which stand at the gate as the three ... ' This is the true God.
When the true God. had emanated, this was his type:

ⲁⲟⲉⲓⲁⲱⲑ.
ⲱⲩⲓⲭⲱⲗ
ⲙⲓⲱ ⲓⲉⲟⲩ
ⲡⲛⲟⲩⲧⲉ ⲛⲧⲁ
ⲗⲏⲑⲓⲁ.

...Jeu the *true* God

When one stood in the treasuries no ranks yet existed.
I stood and called upon the name of my Father so that he should cause other amanations to exist in the treasuries. But he again caused a <power> from himself to move the *true* God.
At first he caused it to radiate within him that he might move his emeanations

36

in the treasuries, that they also might bring forth
emanations, which are those
which he placed as heads over them. But he, the *true* God,
emanated these
from his place. For this reason he gave voice when the
power welled up
within him. This is the first voice which he uttered. He
moved his emanations
until they emanated:

Chapter 7

пєчраи za
ωzzноzazиι
оа . иапасаzаz
иzаиоzаzιа
оиzαιαωzа
єιωzαθθωzα
φωzαиzааᴛо
ⲭ ωzиоzιzω
фаєωzаzωι
враєωιzаzιо
ωⲭ ωzаzаzαι
ⲭ αιωzωφωιа
zаzиотωεz?
фᴛωιzаzаzа
иαι ιc пщоλιⲛт
ιιфᴛλаz.

ιⲉοⲩ ⲱⲱ ⲃ

ⲱⲏⲉ
ⲁⲏⲱ
ιοⲧ
ιⲉοⲩ

ιⲩⲩⲩⲩ

иєⲭар   ачтре-
тоιι   ιιιιι ди-ωаиω
асвоⲩвоⲩ драι ⲛⲟⲩⲧⲩ
ачⲧ ⲛⲧфωⲛⲛ ⲉⲩⲡⲣο-
ⲃаλε ⲉⲃⲟλ ⲉⲧⲉ-ⲧⲁι ⲧⲉ
ⲧϣⲟⲣⲡ ⲡⲣⲟⲃⲟλⲏ.

(Jeu2) His name:	Jeu
	...
	...
	...
	...

	...
	...
	His Character: he caused the

	power to move in.....
	It welled up in him. he gave voice as he emanated
These are the three watchers	This is the first emanation.

These are the ranks which he has caused to be emanated. And there are twelve ranks in each treasury, these being their type: six heads on this side and six on that, turned towards each other. There will be a multitude of ranks standing in them outside these, all of which I will say. There are twelve heads in each rank, and the name belongs to them all, according to rank; this name is that of the twelve ', there being twelve heads in each rank. His name is this: ...

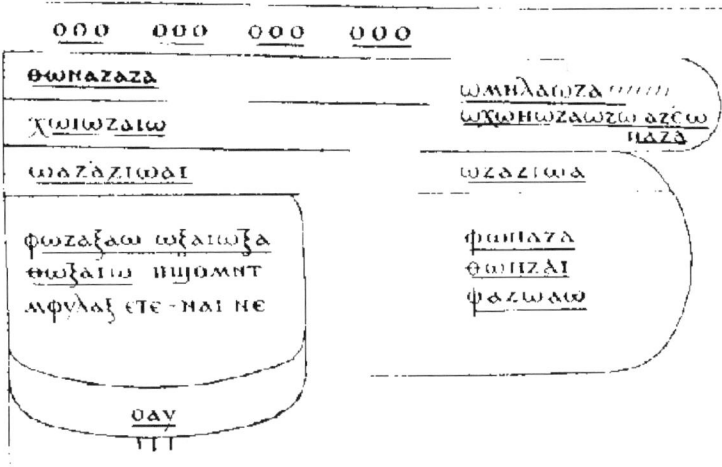

...the three watchers are these

Now the first rank of the treasury is the first which he made as emanation.
I will take for myself twelve out of those ranks and place them so that they serve me.

Chapter 8

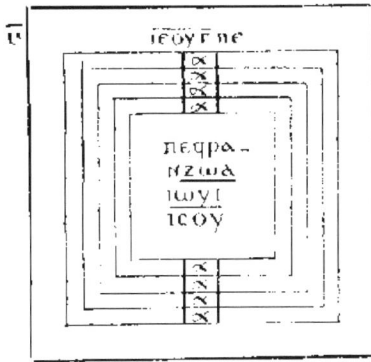

ⲓ̅ⲉ̅ⲟ̅ⲩ̅ ⲅ̅ ⲡⲉ

ⲡⲉϥⲣⲁ-
ⲛⲍⲱⲁ
ⲓⲱⲩⲓ
ⲓⲥⲟⲩ

ⲡⲁⲓ ⲡⲉ ⲡⲉϥⲭⲁⲣⲁⲕⲧⲏⲣ

ⲛⲉϥϥⲩⲗⲁⳅ ⲅⲁⲣ ⲛⲥⲉⲏⲡ
ⲁⲛ ⲉⲛⲧⲁⳅⲓⲥ ⲛⲛⲉⲑⲏⲥⲁⲩⲣⲟⲥ
ⲙⲡⲟⲩⲟⲉⲓⲛ

ⲙⲛⲟⲍⲁⲛⲓⲟⲩⲱ   ⲁⲱ   ⲑⲁ
ⲉⲓⲑⲱⲱⲉⲍⲁ   ⲍⲁⲱ   ⲓⲁ
ϥⲁⲱⲍⲁⲍⲁⲓ   ⲉⲱⲥⲁⲥⲍⲱ
ⲁⲱⲍⲁⲙⲁⲍⲁ   ⲉⲍⲁⲱⲓ
ⲍ(ⲁⲓ)ⲱⲍⲁ
ϥⲁⲍⲁⲍⲁⲓⲱ   ⲛⲉϥϥⲩⲗⲁⳅ
ⲃⲛⲱⲏⲓⲟ   ⲉⲧⲁϩⲉⲣⲁⲧⲟⲩ
ⲛⲁⲥⲁⳅⲁⲥⲁⲓ?   ⲛϩⲟⲩⲛ
ⲑⲱⲛⲁⲥⲁⳅⲉ   ⲛⲙⲡⲩⲗⲏ
                          ⲡⲉ   ⲡⲁⲓ
                          ⲛⲉⲩⲣⲁⲛ
                          ⲓⲱⲍⲁⲁ
                          ⲍⲏⲁⳅⲁⲓ
                          ⲥⲏⲉⲍⲁ?

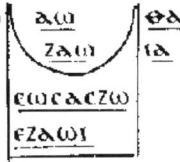

(Jeu 3)	For these watchers do not belong to the ranks of the treasuries of the light
His name	The watchers which stand within the gates are these:

	their names:
...	
	...
Jeu	
	...
This is his character:	
...	

And there are twelve heads in each place of the rank of
every treasury; that is,
these names which are in the places – these names except
for those that will be in them.
These are the three watchers: ....

These are they which ... emanated, when the power
radiated within him.
He emanated twelve emanations, these being his twelve
heads in each emanation,
and this name is that of the twelve according to each one of
the ranks, and these are
one outside the other endlessly. These are the names of the
emanations.

Chapter 9

(Jeu 4)	These are the names of the three watchers:
His name: ... Jeu His Character is this:	These are also the names of the emanations: .

And there are twelve heads in the place of the treasury of his ranks; that is, these names which are in each place; and there are twelve in each rank and this name is that of the twelve, except for those which will be in them, when they sing praises to my Father, so that he gives light-power to them. These are they which ... ' emanated when the power radiated within him. He emanated twelve emanations, there being twelve heads in each emanation, and this name is the twelve, according to each one of the ranks.

And these are one outside the other
endlessly, except for their watchers. The names of the three watchers are: ....

ⲡⲉϥⲣⲁⲛ
ⲩⲓⲱⲑⲓⲱ
ⲓⲉⲟⲩ

ⲡⲉϥⲭⲁⲣⲁⲕⲧⲏⲣ

ⲛⲁⲓ ⲛⲉ ⲡⲅ ⲙⲫⲩⲗⲁⲝ
ⲁⲓⲉ· ⲥⲱⲁⲩ· ⲓⲟⲉⲍⲁ ⲛⲁⲓ
ϩⲱⲱϥ ⲛⲉ ⲛⲉⲡⲣⲟⲃⲟⲗⲟⲥ
ⲟⲩⲉ. ⲓⲱⲁⲑⲏⲥⲁⲁⲍ·
ⲁⲱⲥⲁⲑ?ⲱⲓⲁⲍ· ⲁⲑⲁⲙⲁⲓⲁⲱ·
ⲓⲱⲍⲁⲭⲱⲉ· ⲱⲓⲉⲙⲁⲣⲁ·
ⲱⲱⲱⲁ?ⲁⲍⲁⲓ· ⲁⲉⲑⲏⲓⲁⲱⲍ·
ⲱⲍ?ⲭⲱⲛⲁⲓ· ⲑⲱⲣⲙⲱⲍⲁ·
ⲱⲍⲙⲙⲏⲍⲱⲍ· ⲑⲱⲓⲱⲍⲉⲓⲁ·
ⲍⲁⲉⲗⲭⲱⲍⲁ·

(Jeu 5)	These are the three watchers:
	....
His name:	
....	These are the emanations:
Jeu	....
His character:	

And there are twelve heads in each place of the treasuries of his ranks, that is, these names which are in the places. And there are twelve in each rank, and this name is that of the twelve, except for those that will be in them, when they sing praises to my Father, so that he gives light-power to them. These are they which ... emanated forth from him when the power of my Father radiated within him. He emanated twelve emanations. There are twelve heads in each emanation, and this name is that of the twelve, and there are twelve according to each one of the ranks. And they are one outside the other endlessly, except for the watchers. The three watchers . . . .

Chapter 11 to 34

[The following chapters proceed in very much the same fashion, with similar diagrams and textual comment on the names in the diagrams, up to the Fragment of a Gnostic Hymn. Thereafter the text resumes with fewer diagrams through Chapter 41.]

The Untitled Text in the Bruce Codex

1.

He set him up so that they should strive against the city in
which was their image. And it is in that they move, and in it
that they live. And it is the house of the Father, and the
garment of the Son, and the power of the Mother, and the
image of the Pleroma. This is the First Father of the All.
This is the first eternity. This is the king of unassailables.
This is he in whom the All is unconscious. This is he who
gave form to it within himself. This is the self-originated
and self-begotten place. This is the deep of the All, this is
the great abyss, in truth. This is he to whom the All
reached. There was silence concerning him. He was not
spoken of, for he is an ineffable one, he cannot be
understood. This is the first source. This is he whose voice
has penetrated everywhere. This is the first sound until the
All perceived and understood. This is he whose members
make a myriad myriad powers to each of them.

2.

The second place came into existence which will be called
demiurge and father and logos and source and
understanding mind and man and eternal and infinite. This
is the column, this is the overseer, and this is the Father of
the All. This is he upon whose head the aeons are a crown,
casting forth rays. The circuit of his face is the unknown in
the outer worlds, these who seek after his face at all times,
wishing to know it, for his word has reached them, and they
want to see him. And the light of his eyes penetrates to the
places of the outer pleroma. And the word which comes

from his mouth penetrates what is above and below. And the hair of his head is the number of the hidden worlds, and the boundary of his face is the image of the aeons. The hairs of his face are the number of the outer worlds. And the stretching out of his hands is the manifestation of the cross. The stretching out of the cross is the ennead on the right side and on the left. The sprouting of the cross is the incomprehensible man. This is the Father. This is the source, which wells up from the silence.

This is he who is sought in every place. And this is the Father from whom, like a light-spark, the monad came forth, beside which all the worlds are as nothing. . . . It is this which moved all things with its shining. And they received gnosis and life and hope and rest and love and resurrection and faith and rebirth and the seal. This is the ennead which came from the Father of those without beginning, who alone is Father and Mother unto himself, whose pleroma surrounds the twelve deeps -

1. The first deep is the all-wise from which all sources have come.

2. The second deep is the all-wise from which all the wise have come.

3. The third deep is the all-mystery from which, or out of which, all mysteries have come.

4. The fourth deep moreover is the all-gnosis out of which all gnoses have come.

5. The fifth deep is the all-chaste from which everything chaste has come.

6. The sixth deep is silence. In this is every silence.

7. The seventh deep is the insubstantial door from which all substances has come forth.

8. The eight deep is the forefather from whom, or out of whom, have come into existence all forefathers.

9. The ninth deep moreover is an all-father and a self-farther, that is, every fatherhood is in him and he alone is father to them.

10. The tenth deep is the all-powerful from which has come every power.

11. The eleventh deep moreover is that in which is the first invisible one, from which all invisible ones have come.

12. The Twelfth deep moreover is the truth from which has come all truth.

This is the truth which covers them all. This is the image of the Father. This is the mirror of the All. This is the mother of all the aeons. It is this which surrounds all the deeps. This is the monad which is unknowable or is unknown. This characterless one in which are all characters, which is blessed for ever. This is the eternal Father. This is the ineffable Father : not understood, unthinkable, inaccessible. And they rejoiced, they were glad, they begot myriads upon myriads of aeons in their joy. They were called the births of joy because they rejoiced with the Father. These are the worlds within which the cross grew and Man came into existence out of these incorporeal members. This is the Father and the source of all, whose members are all complete. And every name came into existence from the Father whether unutterable, or imperishable, or unknowable, or invisible, or simple, or still, or power, or all-power, or every name which is in the silence, all of which came into existence from the Father.

It is he whom the outside worlds all, like the stars of the firmament at night, see. As men desire to see the sun, in this way also the outside worlds desire to see him, on account of his invisibility that surrounds him. It is he who at all times gives life to the aeons, and through his word the indivisible one learned to know the monad. And through his word the holy Pleroma came into existence.

3.

This is the Father, the second demiurge. Through the breath of his mouth, the forethought inspired those without existence. They came into being through the will of this one, because it is he who commands the All, so that it comes into existence.

He created the holy Pleroma in this way: four gates with four monads within it, one monad to each gate and six helpers (parastatai) to each gate, and twelve dodecads to each gate, and five pentads of powers to each gate, making 24 helpers (parastatai) ; and 24 myriad powers to each gate, and nine enneads to each gate, and ten decads to each gate, and twelve dodecads to each gate, and five pentads of power to each gate, and an overseer who has three aspects - an unbegotten aspect, a true aspect and an unutterable aspect - to each gate. One of his aspects looks forth from the gate to the outer aeons, the other looks inwards to the Setheus, and the other looks to the height, and the sonship is in each monad. And Aphrêdon is there with his twelve beneficent ones. The forefather is there ; Adam is there, who is of the light, and his 365 aeons; and the perfect mind is there. And they surround a rule (kanôn) which is in immortality. The unutterable aspect of the overseer looks towards to the holy of the holies, that is, the infinite one who is the head of the sanctuary. He has two aspects : one is opened to the place of the deep, and then other is opened to the place of the overseer which is called: the Child. And there is a deep there which is called : the light or the light-giver. And an only-begotten one is concealed within it, who manifests three powers, who is mighty in every power.

This is the indivisible one, this is he who has never divided. This is he to whom the All has opened, for to him the powers belong. He has three aspects : an invisible aspect, and an all-powerful aspect, and an Aphrêdon-aspect which is called Aphrêdon-Pêxos. And there is an only-begotten one concealed within him, namely the triple-powered one. When the thought comes forth from the deep, Aphrêdon takes the thought and brings it to the only-begotten one. The only-begotten one brings it to the Child, and they bring it forth to all the aeons as far as the place of the triple-powered one, and they are completed and taken to the five unbegotten ones.

4.

There is again another place which is called: deep. There
are three fatherhoods within it. The first father there is the
covered one, who is the hidden God. In the second father
there stands five trees, and there is a table in their midst.
And an only-begotten word (logos) stands above the table,
he having the twelve aspects of the mind of the All ; and the
prayer of each one is brought to him. This is he over whom
the All rejoiced because he appeared. And this is he whom
the invisible one strove to know. And this is he on account
of whom the Man was manifested. In the third father there
is the silence (Sigè) and the source; and twelve beneficent
ones look upon it and see themselves in it. And in it is love
and the mind of the All and five seals. And afterwards the
all-mother, in whom the ennead was manifested, whose
names are these: Prôtia, Pandia, Pangenia, Doxophania,
Doxogenia, Doxokratia, Arsenogenia, Lôia, Iouêl.This is the
first unknowable one (akatagnôstos), the mother of the
ennead, which completes a decad from the monad of the
unknowable (agnôstos) one.

5.

After these things there is another place which is broad,
having hidden within it a great wealth which supplies the
All. This is the immeasurable deep. There is a table there, to
which are gathered three greatnesses : a still one, an
unknowable one and an infinite one. There is a sonship in
their midst, which is called Christ the Verifier,. It is he who
verifies each one, and he seals him with the seal of the
Father as he sends them in to the first Father, who exists in
himself. This is he because of whom the All came into

existence, and without whom nothing existed. And this Christ bears twelve aspects : an infinite aspect, an incomprehensible aspect, an unutterable aspect, an simple aspect, an imperishable aspect, a still aspect, an unmoved aspect, an unbegotten aspect and a pure aspect. That place has twelve sources which are called: rational sources, which are filled with eternal life. They are called: deeps, and they are called: the twelve spaces, because they contain all the places of the fatherhood. And the fruit of the All, which they produce, this is the Christ who contains the All.

6.

After all these things is the deep of Setheus which is within them all, and twelve fatherhoods surround him. It is he who is in their midst, and each one of them has three aspects.

The first among them is the indivisible one. He has three aspects ; an infinite aspect, an invisible aspect, and an unutterable aspect. And the second father has an incomprehensible aspect, an unmoved aspect, and an undefiled aspect. The third father has an unknowable aspect, an imperishable aspect, and an aphrêdon aspect. The fourth father has a silence aspect, a source aspect, and an unassailable aspect. The fifth father has a still aspect, an all-powerful aspect, and an unbegotten aspect. The sixth father has an all-father aspect, a self-father aspect, and a progenitor aspect. The seventh father has an all-mystery aspect, an all-wise aspect, and an all-source aspect. The eight father has a light aspect, a rest aspect, and a resurrection aspect. The ninth father has a covered aspect, a first-visible aspect, and a self-begotten aspect. The tenth father has a thrice-male aspect, an Adamas aspect, and a pure aspect. The eleventh father has a triple-powered aspect, a perfect aspect, and a light-spark (Spinther) or spark aspect. The twelfth father has a truth aspect, a forethought aspect and a thought aspect.

These are the twelve fathers which surround the Setheus, making thirty-six in their number. And those that are outside them have received character from them, and because of this they give them glory at all times. Again another twelve surround his head and they have a diadem upon their heads. And they cast rays to the worlds which surround them from the light of the only-begotten one hidden within him, this one whom they seek after.

7.

In order indeed that we should comprehend the subject through those that excel in speaking of these things - as far as we now are concerned - it is not possible that they should be understood in any other way, that is, by us. Indeed, to speak of him with a tongue of flesh, of the manner in which he exists, is an impossibility. For they are great ones who surpass the powers so that they hear through a concept and they follow him except they find a kinsman of theirs in one who can hear of the places from whence he came. For everything follows from its root, because indeed man is a kinsman of the mysteries, because of this he has heard of the mystery. The powers of all the great aeons have given homage to the power which is in Marsanes (Marsianos). They said : "Who is this who has seen these things before his face, that he has thus revealed concerning him?" Nikotheus spoke concerning him; he saw that he was that one. He said : "The Father exists, surpassing every perfection. He has revealed the invisible, triple-powered, perfect one." Each of the perfect men saw him, they spoke of him, giving glory to him, each one in his own way.

This is the only-begotten one hidden in the Setheus ; this is he whom they called the light-darkness.
Because of excess of his light they of themselves alone became dark. This is he through whom the Setheus is king. This is the only-begotten one. There are twelve fatherhoods in his right hand in the type of the twelve apostles. And in his left there are thirty powers. Each one makes twelve, and each possesses two aspects (faces) in the type of the Setheus. One aspect looks to the deep within, the other looks at the triple-powered one. And each one of the fatherhoods in his right hand makes 365 powers according to the word which David spoke, saying : "I will bless the crown of the year in thy beneficence"<Ps 64,1> Now all these powers surround the only-begotten one like a rown, giving light to the aeons in the light of the only-begotten one, as it is written : " In thy light will we see light" <Ps 35> And the only-begotten one is raised above them, as it is written : "The Chariot of God is ten thousandfold"<Ps 67,1>, and again ; "Thousand rejoice, the Lord being in them"<Ps 67,1>.

This is he who dwells in the monad which is in the Setheus. It is this which came forth from the place of which it is not possible to say where it is, which came forth from that which is before the All. This is the Only One. This is he from whom the monad came, like a ship laden with all good things, or like a city filled with every race of man and every king`s image.

This is the manner in which they are all within the monad : there are twelve monads making a crown upon its head ; each one makes twelve. And there are ten decads surrounding its shoulders. And there are nine enneads surrounding its belly. And there are seven hebdomads at its feet, and each one makes a hebdomad. And to the veil which surrounds it like a tower, there are twelve gates. There are twelve myriad powers at each gate, and they are called archangels and also angels.

This is the mother-city of the only-begotten one. This is the only-begotten of whom Phosilampes spoke : "He exists before the All" It is he who came forth from the endless, characterless, patternless and self-begotten aeon who has begotten himself, who came forth from the ineffable and immeasurable one, who exists verily and truly. It is he in whom exists the truly existent one; that is to say, the incomprehensible Father exists in his only-begotten Son. The All rests in the ineffable and unutterable, unruled and untroubled one, of whose godhood which is itself no godhood, no one is able to speak. And when Phosilampes understood, he said : "Those things which verily and truly exist and those which do not exist are for his sake. This is he for whose sake are those that truly exist which are secret, and those that do not truly exist which are manifest."

This truly is the only-begotten God. This is he whom the All knew. They became God, and they raised up his name : God. This is he of whom John spoke: "In the beginning was the Word and the Word was with God and the Word was God. This one without whom nothing exist, and that which has come into existence in him is life"<John 1.1,3,4>

This is the only-begotten one in the monad,. Dwelling in it like a city. And this is the monad which is in Setheus like a concept. This is Setheus who dwells in the sanctuary like a king, and he is as God. This is the creative Word which commands the All that they should work. This is the creative Mind, according to the command of God the Father. This is he to whom the creation prays as God, and as Lord, and as Saviour, and as one to whom they have submitted themselves. This is he at whom the All marvels because of his beauty and comeliness. This is he whom the All - those within being a crown upon his head, and those outside at his feet, and those of the midst surrounding him - bless, saying ; "Holy, Holy, Holy art Thou, Thou art living within those that live, thou art holy within the holy ones, thou dost exist within those that exist, and thou art the father within the fathers, and thou art God within the gods, and thou art Lord within the lords, and thou art a place within all the places"

And they bless him, saying :"Thou art the house, and thou art the dweller in the house." And they bless him again, saying to the Son who is hidden within him : "Thou art existent, thou art the only-begotten one, the light and the life and the grace (Charis)"

8.

Then Setheus sent the light-spark to the indivisible one. And it shone, it gave light to the whole place of the holy pleroma. And they saw the light of the light-spark. They rejoiced and they gave myriads of myriads of glories to the Setheus and to the light-spark which had manifested, as they saw that all their likeness was in him. And they depicted the light-spark within them as a man of light and truth.

They called him one assuming all forms, and pure one, and they called him unmoved one, and all the aeons called him all-powered one. This is the servant of the aeons and he serves the Pleroma.

And the indivisible one sent the light-spark out of the pleroma. And the triple-powered one came down to the places of the self-begotten one. And they saw the grace of the aeons of the light which was granted to them. They rejoiced because he who exists came forth among them.

Then the veils opened, and the light penetrated down to the matter below and to those who had no form and no likeness. And in this way they acquired the likeness of the light. Some indeed rejoiced because the light came to them and they became rich. Others wept because they became poor, and those things which they had were taken away. And this is the way it happened to the grace which came forth. Therefore captivity was taken captive. They gave honour to the aeons which had received the light-spark. Watchers were sent to them, namely Gamaliel, Strempsuchos, Agramas and those with him. They became helpers to those who believed in the light-spark.

9.

And in the place of the indivisible one there are twelve springs, and upon them twelve fatherhoods, surrounding the indivisible one in the manner of the deeps or these veils. And there is a crown upon the indivisible one in which is every species of life : and every triple-powered species; and every incomprehensible species : and every endless species ; and every unutterable species; and every silent species ; and every unmoved species ; and every first-visible species ; and every self-begotten species ; and every true species ; all being within it.

And in this is every species and every gnosis. And every power receives light from it.

And every mind is revealed in it.

This is the crown which the Father of the All gave to the indivisible one, in which there are 365 species, and they shine and fill the All with imperishable and inextinguishable light.

This is the crown which gives power to every power. And this is the crown for which all the immortal ones pray. And from this will those who have first manifested in the will of the unknowable one, on the day of rejoicing give to the invisible one, namely the foremost one, the all-divine one, and the all-begetting one, they and their fellows. And after the invisible one, all the aeons will receive their crowns from it and hasten forth with the indivisible one. And the All will receive their completion through the imperishable one. And for this reason do those who have received bodies pray, wishing to leave their bodies behind, and to receive the crown which is laid up for them in the imperishable aeon. And this is the indivisible one which has created the contest for the All.

And all things were granted to it through him who is superior to all things. And to it was granted the immeasurable deep, in which the fatherhoods cannot be numbered. And its enneads is without character,. And the characters of the whole creation are in it, as its ennead makes twelve enneads, and a place is in its midst which is called the god-bearing or god-begetting land.

This is the land of which it has been said : "He who tills his land shall be satisfied with bread, and shall enlarge his threshing floor." <Proverbs 12.11> and also "The king of the filed that has been tilled is over all"<Eccl. 5.9> And all these powers which are in this god-begetting land receive crowns upon their heads. By this means the Paralemptores are known, because of the crowns upon their heads, whether or not they are from the indivisible one.

And moreover there is in it the all-mother. In it there are seven wisdoms and nine enneads and ten decads. And there is a great rule (kanôn) in their midst. And there is a great invisible one standing upon it, and a great unbegotten one and a great incomprehensible one. Each one has three faces. And the prayer and the blessing and the song of praise of the creation mount above that rule which is in the midst of the all-mother, and in the midst of the seven wisdoms, and in the midst of the nine enneads and the ten decads. And all these stand above the rule, fulfilled in the fruit of the aeons.

This (is what) the only-begotten one hidden in the indivisible one, before whom there is a source which twelve beneficent ones surround, commands them. And each one has a crown upon his head, and he has twelve powers which surround him. And they bless the only-begotten king, saying :

"For thy sake we have worn the glory, and through thee we have seen the Father of the All, ... and the Mother of all things, who is hidden in every place who is the thought of every aeon.

And she is the concept of every god and every lord. And she is the gnosis of every invisible one. And thy image is the mother of every incomprehensible one. And it is the power of every infinite one" And they bless the only-begotten one, saying : "Through thy image we have seen thee, we have fled to thee, we have stood with thee, we have received the unfading crown, which has been known through thee. Glory to thee for ever, O only begotten one" And they all said : "Amen" at once.

And he became a light-body. He passed through the aeons of the indivisible one, until he reached the only-begotten one who is in the monad, who continues in quietness or in stillness. And he received the grace of the only-begotten one, which is his Christhood, and he received the eternal crown. This is the Father of all the light-sparks. And this is the head of every immortal body. And this is he for whose sake resurrection of the limbs were granted.

10.

But outside the indivisible one and outside his characterless ennead, in which are all characters, there are three other enneads, and each one makes nine enneads. And within each one there is a rule, to which three fatherhoods ' are gathered: an infinite one, an unutterable one and an incomprehensible one. And in the midst of the second (ennead) there is a rule, and there are three fatherhoods in it: an invisible one, an unbegotten one and an unmoved one. Also in the third (ennead) there is a rule, and there are three fatherhoods in it: a still one, an unknowable one, and a triple- powered one. And through these the All has known God.

And they fled to him and they begot a multitude of aeons which cannot be numbered. And according to each ennead they make myriads upon myriads of glories. And each ennead has a monad within it. And in each monad there is a place which is called imperishable, which is the holy land. In the land of each of these monads there is a source. And there are myriads upon myriads of powers receiving crowns upon their heads from the crown of the triple-powered one. And in the midst of' the enneads and in the midst of the monads is the immeasurable deep. And the All, those within and those without, looks forth upon it. And twelve fatherhoods are

1. The first fatherhood is an infinite aspect, and thirty powers surround it which are infinite.

2. The second fatherhood is an invisible aspect, and thirty invisible ones surround it

3. The third fatherhood is an incomprehensible aspect, and thirty incomprehensible ones surround it.

4. And the fourth fatherhood is an invisible aspect. Thirty invisible powers surround it.

5. The fifth fatherhood ' is an all-powered aspect, and thirty all-powered ones surround it.6. The sixth fatherhood is an all-wise aspect, and thirty all-wise ones surround it.

7. The seventh fatherhood is an unknowable aspect. And thirty unknowable powers surround it.

8. The eighth fatherhood is a still aspect, and thirty still powers surround it.

9. The ninth fatherhood is an unbegotten aspect, and thirty unbegotten powers surround it.

10. The tenth fatherhood is an unmoved aspect, and thirty unmoved powers surround it.

11. The eleventh fatherhood is an all-mystery aspect, and thirty all-mystery powers surround it.

12. The twelfth fatherhood is a triple-powered aspect, and thirty triple-powered powers surround it.

And in the midst of the immeasurable deep there are five powers which are called by these unutterable names:

1. The first is called love', from which all love has come.

2. The second (is called) hope, through which the only-begotten Son of God was hoped in.

3. The third is called faith', through which the mysteries of the ineffable have been believed in.

4. The fourth is called gnosis, through which the first father has been known, he because of whom they exist, and through whom has been known the mystery of the silence, which speaks in all things, which is hidden - the first monad,

for whose sake the All became insubstantial. This is the mystery on whose head the 365 substances' are a crown like the hair of a man. And the holy pleroma is like these footstools under his feet. This is the door of God.

5. The fifth is called peace, through which peace was given to all those within and those without, because in it was the All created.

This is the immeasurable deep in which are the 365 fatherhoods '.

And the year was divided by means of these. This is the deep which surrounds the holy pleroma from without. This is that

upon which is the triple-powered one with its branches like these trees. And this is that over which is Musanios ', with all those that belong to him. And Aphredon is there with his twelve beneficent ones. And a rule is in their midst (to which) are brought the blessings and the songs of praise and the supplications and the prayers of the mother of all things' or the mother of the All, who is called Manifest. And they are given form through the twelve beneficent ones. They are sent forth by it to the pleroma of Setheus. They remember these things in the outer eon in which is the matter. This is the deep from which the triple-powered one received glory until he reached the indivisible one. And he received the grace of the unknowable one, from which he received the sonship of such greatness 4 that the pleroma was not able to bear it, because of the abundance of its light and the shining within it.

11.

And the whole pleroma was agitated, and the deep with all those within it moved, and they fled to the eon of the mother.

And the mystery commanded that the veils of the aeons be drawn back until the overseer established the aeons again. And the overseer established the aeons again, as it is written: "He established the inhabited world and it shall not be moved "; and also: "The earth was dissolved with all those upon it." And then the triple-powered one in whom the Son was hidden came forth, and on his head was the crown of stability, making myriads upon myriads of glories, and those who cry out: "Make straight the way of the Lord and receive the grace of God. And he will fill all the aeons which belong to you (?) ' with the grace of the only-begotten Son." And the holy Father, the all-perfect one, stood over the immeasurable deep. And it is he from whom is the whole fullness: "Out of his fullness have we received grace." Then the aeon was established, it ceased to move. The Father established it so that it should not move for ever. And the aeon of the mother remained filled with those things which were in it, until the command came forth through the mystery hidden in the first Father - from whom the mystery came forth - that his Son should establish the All once again in his gnosis, in which the All is contained'.

Then Setheus sent a creative word with which were many powers having crowns upon their heads. And their crowns sent forth rays, and the shining of their bodies enlivened ' the place to which they came. And the word which came forth from their mouths was eternal life. And the light which came forth from their eyes was to them rest. And the movement of their hands was their flight to the place from whence they came forth. And their looking into their faces was the gnosis in relation to themselves. And their journey to themselves was their turning inwards once again.

And the stretching out of their hands was their setting up. And the hearing of their ears was the perception which is in their hearts.

And the uniting of their members was the gathering together of the dispersed of Israel. And the holding of them was their fixing to the word. And the cipher which was in their fingers was the number or reckoning which came forth according to what is written: "He who numbers the multitudes of stars and gives names to them all*." And the whole unity of the creative word happened with those that came in the movement which happened.

And they all became one, as it is written: "They all became one in the one and only One '." And then this creative word became a power of God, and Lord and Saviour and Christ and king and good and father and mother. This is he whose work was of worth. He received honour, and he became father of those who have believed. This became law in Aphredonia, and mighty.

12.

And the all-visible one came forth wearing the crown, and gave (crowns) to those who have believed. And the mother, the virgin and the power ' of the aeons, gave rank ' to her worlds according to the ordinance of the inner. And she laid

67

therein the light-spark according to the type of the monad. And she placed the covering surrounding it, and she placed the forefather in the type of the indivisible one and the twelve beneficent ones surrounding him. There were crowns upon them, and a seal of glory on their right, and a (source) in their midst. And a triple-powered aspect in the source, and a rule with twelve fathers and a sonship hidden within them surrounding it.

And she set up the self-father in the type (of the)characterless ennead. And she gave to him authority over everyone, he being father to himself alone. And she crowned him with every glory.

And she gave to him love and peace and truth, and myriads of powers, so that he should gather together those that were scattered in the agitation which happened at the time when the triple- powered one came forth, with the joy and the Lord of the All, who has power to give life and to destroy.

And she set up the protogenitor son ' in the type of the triple- powered one. And she gave to him a ninefold ennead. And she gave ten times five decads, so that he should be able to complete the contest which was given ' to him. And she gave to him the first-fruits of the sonship in which he was able to become triple- powered. And he received the promise of the sonship whereby the All was given over ' (to him). And he received the contest which was entrusted to him. And he raised up all the purity of the matter, and made it a world and an aeon and a city which is called imperishability and Jerusalem. And it is also called "the new earth ". And it is also called "self-complete." And it is also called "unruled." And furthermore that earth is a god-bearing and a life-giving one.

It is this for which the mother asked, that it be set up. Because of this she placed ordinance and rank, and she placed forethought and love in this earth. This is the earth about which it has been written: "The earth which drinks rain-water many times ", that is, which increases light in itself many times from its going forth to its coming in. This is what has been (written) concerning the man with sense-perception: "And he was typified and created in the type of this land." This it is that the protogenitor saved by means of his own power '.

Because of this work, the Father of the All (pl.), the indescribable one ', sent a crown in which is the name of the All (pl.) ', whether endless, or unutterable, or incomprehensible, or imperishable, or unknowable, or still, or all-powered, or indivisible. This is the crown of which it is written: "It was given to Solomon on the day of the joy of his heart." The first monad furthermore sent him an ineffable garment ' which was all light and all life and all resurrection, and all love and all hope and all faith and all wisdom, and all gnosis, and all truth, and all peace, and all-visible ', and all-mother, and all-mystery, and all-source, and all-perfect, and all invisible, and all unknowable, and all endless, and all unutterable, and all deep, and all incomprehensible, and all pleroma, and all silence, and all unmoved, and all unbegotten, and all still, and) all monad, and all ennead, and all dodecad, and all ogdoad, and all decad, and all hebdomad, and all hexad, and all pentad, and all tetrad, and all triad, and all dyad, and all monad.

And the All is in it, and also all found themselves ' in it, and knew themselves in it. And it (the monad) gave light to them all with its ineffable light. Myriads upon myriads of powers were given to it, so that at one (and the same) time it should establish the All. It gathered its garments and made them into the form of a veil which surrounded it on all sides. And it poured itself over them all, it raised them all. And it divided them all according to rank and according to ordinance and according to forethought.

13.

And then the existent separated itself from the non-existent.

And the non-existent is the evil which has manifested in matter.

And the enveloping power separated those that exist from those that do not exist. And it called the existent "eternal", and it called the non-existent "matter". And in the middle it separated ' those that exist from those that do not Exist, and it placed veils between them. And it placed purifying powers so that they should purify and cleanse them. And it gave ordinance to those that exist in this way. And it placed the mother as head. And it gave to her ten aeons, there being a myriad powers in each aeon, and a monad and an ennead in each aeon.

And it placed in her an all-womb, And it gave to her a power so that she should place it hidden within her, so that no one should know it. And it placed in her a great rule with three powers standing by it: an unbegotten one, an unmoved one, and the great pure one. And it gave to it (the rule) twelve others which were crowned and surrounded it. And it gave to it (the rule) seven other commanders who had the all-perfect seal, and a crown upon their heads with twelve adamantine ' stones in it, which were from Adamas, the Man of Light '. And it set up the forefather in the aeons of the mother of all things. It gave to him all the authority of fatherhood, and it gave to him powers that they should obey him as father, and as first father of all that had come into existence. And it placed on his head a crown of twelve species.

And it gave to him a power which is triple-powered and all-powered.

And it gave to him the sonship, and myriads upon myriads of glories. And it gave them to him. And it surrounded him with the pleroma. And it gave to him the authority to make all things live and perish. And it gave to him a power out of the aeon which is called Solmistos ', him whom all the aeons seek, whence he manifested. And myriads upon myriads of glories were given to him and the aeons with him. Moreover the power that was given to the forefather is called first-visible because it is he who was first manifest. And he was called unbegotten because no one had created him. And he was (called) the ineffable and the nameless one. And he was also called self-begotten and self-willed because he had revealed himself by his own will. And he was called self- glorified because he was manifest with the glories which he possessed. He was called invisible because he is hidden and is not seen.

And it (the enveloping power) gave to him another power, which from the beginning had revealed the light-spark in this same place, and which was called by holy and all-perfect names.

The first is protia ', that is, the foremost. It is called pandia, namely that which exists in all things '. It is called pangenia, namely that which has begotten all things. It is called doxogenia because it is the begetter of glory. Furthermore it is called doxophania because it is the revealer of glory. It is also called doxokratia because it rules over the glory. It is also called arsenogenia which is the begetter of males. It is also called loia, of which the interpretation is: God with us. It is also called iouel, of which the interpretation is: God for ever. But that which commanded these powers to manifest is called phania, of which the interpretation is: the revelation. And the angel which was revealed with them is called by the glories doxogenes and doxophanes, of which the interpretation is: the begetter of glory and the revealer of glory, because he is one of these glories which stand surrounding the great power. And he is called doxokrator ', that is, at his manifestation he ruled over great glories.

14.

These are the powers which were given to the forefather who was placed in the aeon of the mother. And there were given to him myriads upon myriads of glories, and angels and archangels and ministers, so that those that are of matter should serve him '. And he was given authority over all things. And he :created a great aeon for himself. And he placed in it a great pleroma and a great sanctuary. And he placed within it all the powers which he had received. And he rejoiced with them, as he begot his creations once again, in accordance with the command of the Father hidden in the silence who had sent to him these riches. And the crown of fatherhood was given to him, because he had set him up as Father of those who had come into existence after him.

And then he cried out, saying; "My children with whom I am in travail until the Christ take form in you." And again he cried ' out: "For I am ready now to place a single husband, Christ, beside a holy Virgin." But since he saw the grace which the hidden Father gave to him, he, the forefather, wished to turn the All towards the hidden father, for his wish is this, that the All should turn to him.

And when the mother saw these great things that were given to her forefather, she rejoiced greatly. And she was glad. Because of this she said ': "My heart has rejoiced and my tongue has been glad." Afterwards she cried out to the endless power which stands with the hidden aeon of the Father, which belongs to the great powers of glory and which) is called among the glories thrice-born
, that is, the one who was begotten three times, which is also called thrice-begotten ' and is also called Hermes (?). And she also prayed ' to the one hidden from all things, that he send to the mother what she needed. And the hidden Father sent to her the mystery which covers all the aeons and all the glories, which has an all-perfect, that is, a complete crown. And he placed it on the head of the great invisible one who was hidden within her, who is imperishable and is unbegotten and the great power with him which is called begetting-males, which will fill all the aeons with glory. And in this way the All will receive the crown through him.

15.

And afterwards she set up the eternal self-father. And she
gave to him the aeon of the covered ones in which is the All:
the species with the forms, and the likenesses with the
forms, and the changes ', and the differences with the four
changes, and the number with the numbered, and the
knower with the known. And she placed him so that he
should cover over all things that are within him, and so that
he should give to him that asks him. And she gave to him
ten powers and nine enneads and a pentad of aeons.
Luminaries were given to him. And authority was given to
him over all the hidden things, so that he would give grace
to those who had striven.

And they fled from the matter of the aeon, leaving it behind
them. And they fled to the aeon of the self-father and they
received the promise which was made to them through him
who said: "He who will leave father and mother and brother
and sister and wife and child and possessions, and bear his
cross and follow me', will receive the promised things which
I have promised to him. And I will give to them the mystery
of my hidden Father because they have loved what is theirs,
and they have fled from him who persecutes them with
violence".

And he gave to them praise and joy and gladness and
pleasure and peace and hope and faith and love and truth
which does not change. And this is the ennead which was
granted to those who fled from the matter. And they
became blessed and they became perfect, and they knew the
true God. And they understood the Mystery which became
Man, why he was revealed, until they saw him who is indeed

an invisible one; and that he wrote his Word concerning him until they knew him, and fled to him and became divine and perfect.

16.

Afterwards the mother established her first-born son. She gave to him the authority of the sonship. And she gave to him hosts of angels and archangels. And she gave to him twelve powers to serve him. And she gave to him a garment' in which to accomplish all things. And in it were all bodies: the body of fire, and the body of water, and the body, of air and the body of earth, and the body of wind, and the body (of angels), and the body of archangels, and the body of powers, and the body of mighty ones, id the body of gods, and the body of lords. In a word, within it ere all bodies so that none could hinder him from going to the :eight or from going down to the abyss.

And this is the protogenitor, to whom those within and those without promised all that he would desire. And this is he who divided all matter. And in the manner in which he spread himself' out over it "like a bird which stretches forth its wings over its eggs," thus he, the protogenitor, did to the matter. And he raised up myriads upon myriads of kinds or species. When the matter became warm it released the multitude of powers which were with him. And they grew like vegetation, and they were divided' according to species and according to kinds. And he gave law to them to love one another and to honour God and to bless him, and to seek him - who he is and what he is - and that they should marvel at the place from which they came, that it is narrow and difficult, and that they should not return to it again, but follow after him who gave law to them.

And he brought them forth from the darkness of the matter which was mother to them, and be said to them that light existed because they did not yet know light, whether it existed or not.

Then he gave to them the commandment not to do harm to one another. He went forth from them to the place of the mother of the All with the forefather and the self-father, so that they should give ordinance to those that came forth from the matter.

17.

And the mother of the All and the forefather and the self-father and the protogenitor and the powers of the aeon of the mother sang a great song of praise, blessing the One Alone, saying: "Thou alone art the infinite one, thou alone art the deep, and thou alone art the unknowable one. And thou art he for whom everyone seeks, and they do not find ' thee, for none can know thee without thy will, and none can bless thee without thy will '. And thy will alone is that which became place for thee, for none can become place for thee because to all thou art their place '. I pray thee to give ranks to those of the world, and to give ordinances to my offspring according to thy pleasure. And do not cause sorrow to my offspring, because no one has ever been made sorrowful through thee, and no one has known thy counsel. Thou art he whom all those within and those without lack. For thou alone art an incomprehensible one, thou alone art the invisible one, and thou alone art the insubstantial one, and thou alone art he who has given character to all creation. Thou hast manifested them in thyself. Thou art the demiurge of those that have not yet manifested - these which thou alone knowest, and we do not know them. Thou alone art he who gives signs of them to us, so that we should ask of thee concerning them, that thou shouldst manifest them, and we should know them through thee alone. Thou alone didst bring thyself to the measure of the hidden worlds, until the knew thee. It is thou who hast given to them to know that it I thou who hast borne them in thy incorporeal body. And thou ha! created them, for thou hast begotten Man in thy self-originate mind, and in the thought and the perfect idea. This is Man, begotten of mind (nous) ', to whom thought gave form. It is thou who hast given all things to Man. And he has worn them like garment.

and he has put them on like clothing, and he has wrapped himself in the creation like a mantle. This is Man whom the All prays to know. Thou alone hast commanded Man that he be revealed so that they know thee through him, that thou hast begotten him. And thou wast revealed according to thy will. Thou art he to whom I pray, 0 Father of all fatherhoods, and God of all.

gods, and Lord of all lords. Thou art he whom I beseech to give ranks to my kinds and my offspring, these to whom I gave abundance in thy name and in thy power. Thou only Sovereign and thou only changeless one, give me power and I will cause my offspring to know thee, that thou art their Saviour."

18.

And when the mother ceased praying to the infinite an unknowable one who fills the All and gives life to them all, he heard her and all those with her who belong to her. And he sent to her a power from the Man whom they desire to see. And from the infinite one came the infinite light-spark, at which the aeons wondered where he was hidden before he revealed himself through the infinite Father. This one who had revealed the All in himself, where was he hidden? And the powers of the hidden aeons followed him until they came to him who is revealed, and until they reached the holy pleroma. And he concealed himself in the powers of those who came forth from the hidden one. And he made them into a world. He wore it (the world) in the holy (place). And the powers of the pleroma saw him, they loved him.

They blessed him in songs of praise which were ineffable ' and unutterable by tongues of flesh, and which were reflected on by the Man within himself. And he received their song of praise, he made it into a veil for their worlds, surrounding them like a wall.

And he came forth to the limits of the mother of the All. He stood upon the universal aeon.

19.

And the All was moved in the presence of the Lord of the whole earth. And the aeon was agitated and it remained so because it saw him whom it did not know. And the Lord of Glory lowered himself'. He separated the matter. He made it into two parts and two lands. And he set boundaries to each land. And he told them that they were from one father and one mother.

And those that fled to him worshipped him. He gave to them the land on the right side of him, and he granted to them eternal life and immortality. And he called (the land) on the right side "the land of life," and that on the left ' "the land of death." ' And he called the land on the right side "the land of light," and that on the left "the land of darkness." ' And he called the land on the right side "the land of rest," and the land on the left "the land of toil." And he set boundaries between them, and veils between them, so that they should not see one another. And he placed watchers upon their veils. And he gave many honours to those who had worshipped him. And he exalted them over those who had opposed him and withstood him. And he spread out the land on the right side into many lands. And he made them each into ranks, and each into aeons, and each into worlds, and each into heavens ', and each into firmaments, and each into heavens, and each into places', and each into places, and each into spaces. And he appointed laws for them. He gave to them commandments: "Abide in my word and I will give to you eternal life '. And I will send you powers. And I will strengthen you with spirits of power, and I will give you authority as you will.

And no one will prevent you in what you wish. And you will beget for yourselves aeons and worlds and heavens, (so that) the intelligible spirits come and dwell in them. And you will become gods, and you will know that you are from God, and you will see him, that he is God within you, And he will dwell in your aeon." And the Lord of the All said these words to them. And he withdrew from them and concealed himself from them '.

20.
And those begotten of matter rejoiced because they were remembered. And they rejoiced that they had come forth from what is narrow and painful, and they begged the hidden mystery: "Give authority to us so that we make for ourselves aeons and worlds, according to thy word which thou 0 Lord hast established with thy servant. For thou alone art the unchanging one. And thou alone art the infinite one. And thou alone art the incomhensible one. And thou alone art the unbegotten one, and the self-begotten one and the self-father. And thou alone art the unmoved one and the unknowable one. And thou alone art the silence and the love and the source of the All. And thou alone art the immaterial and the undefiled one; and the ineffable one with regard to his generation, and the unthinkable one with regard to his revelation. Now hear me, 0 imperishable Father and immortal Father, thou God of the hidden things and thou only light and life, thou alone invisible and thou alone unutterable and thou alone undefiled, and thou alone invincible, and thou) alone the first- existent, the One before whom there is none, Hear our prayer with which we have prayed to him who is hidden in all places. Hear us and send to us incorporeal spirits that they may dwell with us and teach us those things which thou hast promised to us, and that they may dwell in us and that we become bodies to them. Because it is thy will that this should happen, let it happen. And give ordinance to our work and set it up according to thy will and according to the ordinance of the hidden aeons. And thou only art ordinance to us, for we are thine."

And he heard them, he sent powers of discernment which know the ordinance of the hidden aeons. He sent them forth according to the ordinance of the hidden ones. And he established ranks according to the ranks of the height, and according to the hidden ordinance. They began from below upwards, in order that the building should join together; And he created the land of air ', the dwelling-place of those that come forth, that they should remain upon it until the establishment of those below them.

Next (is) the true dwelling-place. Within this the place of repentance. Within this the antitypes of erodes. Next the sojourning as stranger ', the repentance.Within this the self-begotten antitypes. In that place they are immersed in the name of the self-begotten one who is God over them. And in that place over the source of living water were put powers which were brought forth as they came. These are the names of the powers which are over the living water: Michar and Micheu '. And they are purified through Barpharanges '. And within these <are> the aeons of the Sophia. Within these (is) truth in verihood, The Pistis Sophia 'is there, and the pre-existent living Jesus ', and the aerodioi and the twelve aeons. In that place were put Sellao, Eleinos, Zogenethles, Selmelche, and the self-begotten one of the aeons. And within it were placed four lights Eleleth, Daveide, Oroiael, [Harmozel] ...

(lacuna)

(From this point until the end, several unplaced leaves are appended to the text:)

21

.... (incomprehensible, they have not comprehended him (as> Father of the All (pl.) and also (as> ... of the All (pl.) and as ... of all (pl.) these, and insubstantial, invisible, unknown, infinite <and> unknowable, in<comprehensible) in his un(attainable>, unapproachable image. And his boundary is within it <the image?> ... in it in this way (that it) sets bounds to them all in its incorporeality. It sets bounds to them all in incorporeality and in insubstantiality. This is the ineffable, unutterable, unknowable, invisible, immeasurable and infinite Father. He, of himself within himself, has brought himself to the measure ' of those within him.

And he has brought the thought of his greatness to the measure of insubstantiality, until he has made them insubstantial. For he is an incomprehensible one. Through his members he has, of himself', made a place for his members, that they should dwell in it and know that he is their Father, and that it is he who has emanated them in his first concept: this which became a place for them, and made them insubstantial so that they should know him. For he was unknown by all. This became ' his ... of light in the form (of a)... and in the form (of a) ... and in the form of a ... (giving)... to them in the (thought)) of his greatness .

He has brought <them forth) in his thought. His members <became) insubstantial, But <they) were <incomprehensible> to this place.

82

Each one of <them made) a myriad in his members, (and) each one of them saw him <as the> Son that he was completed <in him>.

And the Father sealed him as his Son within them, so that they should know him within themselves. And the name moved them within themselves to make them see the invisible (and) unknowable one. And they gave glory to the Only One and to the concept within him, and to the intelligible word. And so they gave glory to the three which are one, because through him they have become insubstantial. And the Father took their whole likeness.

He made it into a city or a man '. He portrayed the All (pl.) in him, namely all these powers. Each one of them knew him in this city.

Each one gave myriads of glories to the man or the city of the Father who is in the All. And [the Father took] the glory. He made it into a garment outside the man who...

(lacuna of one page)... within him. And he made his belly in the type of the holy pleroma. And he made his nerves going out from one another in the type of a hundred myriad of powers, less four myriads.

And he made the twenty digits in the likeness of the two decads ': the hidden decad and the manifest decad. And he made the navel of his belly in the likeness of the monad' hidden in the Setheus.

He made the large intestine in the likeness of the Setheus who is lord over the pleroma. And he made the small intestine in the likeness of the ennead ... of the Setheus. And he made his womb in the type of the interior of the holy pleroma ...

(lacuna of two lines) ... and he made (his) knees in the type of the still one and the unknowable one who serve the All, and they rejoice with those who will be saved. And he made his members in the type of the deep in which are 365 fatherhoods ', according to the type of the fatherhoods ... <and> he made the hair of his body in the type o the worlds of the pleroma. And he filled him with wisdom like the all-wise one. And he filled him with mysteries within, in the manner of the Setheus. And he filled him outwardly in the manner of the indivisible one. And he made him incomprehensible in the type of the incomprehensible one who is in every place, who is the Only One in the All and who is not comprehended. And he made him surrounding another in the type of the covering which clothes the hidden mysteries. And he made his <right> foot ' the type of the indivisible one, (and it was called) right foot.

(And he made the> four corners ' in the type of the four gates.

And he made the two thighs in the type of the myriarchs which are on the right and on the left. And he made his necessities (genitals) in the type of those that go forth and those that come in. And he made his two hips in (the type of the> silence... .

... <and> he made the ... within it', (one in the> type of Aphredon, the other in the type of Musanios. And he made ... his feet, the right (foot) in the type of the all-visible one,

and the left foot in the type of the mother beneath all
things.

22.

And this is the Man who was made according to each aeon '.
And this is he whom the All desired (to know). This is the
all-perfect one, and this is the God-man who himself is a
god '.

And he is an invisible one, and an unknowable one, and an
all- still one, and an incomprehensible one"and an unmoved
one. He whom it is not possible to curse, it is only possible
to bless ', saying: "I bless thee, 0 Father of all fathers of
light. I bless thee, 0 infinite one of light, who surpassest all
that is infinite. I bless thee, 0 incomprehensible one of light,
who art above all that is incomprehensible. I bless thee, 0
unutterable one of light who art before all that is
unutterable. I bless thee, 0 imperishable one of light (who)
surpassest all that is imperishable.

<I bless> thee 0 (source of light whence is all) light. I bless
(thee), 0 <ineffable one) of light. (I bless> thee, 0
unthinkable one of light <itself). I bless thee, 0 unbegotten
one of (light). I bless thee, 0 self-(existent) one of light. I
bless (thee>, 0 forefather of light, <who) surpassest all
forefathers. (I bless> thee, 0 invisible one of light, who art
before (all) that is invisible. (I) bless thee, 0 thought of
light, who surpassest all thoughts. I bless thee, 0 God of
Light, who art before all gods. I bless thee, 0 gnosis that art
light to all gnoses. I bless thee, 0 unknowable one of light,
who art before all that is unknowable. I bless thee, 0 still
one of light, who art before all that is still. I bless <thee>, 0

all-powered one of light, who surpasseth all that is all-powered. I bless thee, triple-powered one of light, who surpassest all that is triple- powered. I bless thee, O indivisible one of light, but thou art he who divides all light. I praise thee, O pure one of light, who surpassest all the pure ones. I bless thee...

(lacuna of three lines)

as thou speakest ... I bless thee, thou who understandest all, while (no one) understands thee. I bless (thee, thou who) enclosest : All, while (no one) encloses thee. (I bless) thee, thou who begotten hast begotten all (because) no one has begotten thee.

',bless) thee, O source of the All (and of) all things. I bless (thee), O truly self-begotten one of light, who art before (all) the self-begotten ones. I bless thee, O truly unmoved one of light, thou (light) to those who have moved in thy (light), I bless thee, O silence of all silences of the light. I bless thee, O Saviour of (all) saviours of the light, I bless (thee), O only incomprehensible one of light. I bless thee, who alone art place of all places of the All. I bless (thee), who alone art wise and who alone art wisdom.

I bless (thee), O only all-mystery. (I) bless thee, O only all-perfect one of (light). I bless thee, O only unattainable one....

(lacuna of two lines)

... <I bless> thee, O good one, <who dost manifest all> good things, I bless thee, O light, who alone dost manifest (all lights). I bless <thee>, thou who arousest (all) understanding, who givest life to all souls. <I bless thee>, O rest of those... (I) bless thee ', thou who dwellest (in) every fatherhood from the (beginning) until now. They seek for (thee), for thou art their (quest).

O hear the prayer of (the man?) in every place who <prays with) his whole heart.

This is the (Father) of every father, and (the God) of every god, and <the Lord> of every lord, and <the Son> of all sons, (and) the Saviour of (all) saviours, and the invisible one of all that is invisible, and <the silence> of all silences, and <the> infinite one of all that is infinite, and the incomprehensible one of all that is incomprehensible, and <the> abyss-dweller of all abyss-dwellers, and a place of all places. The one and only intelligible one who exists before <all> mind; and furthermore, is mind before all mind, (and is an) incomprehensible one (who comprehends all), and one without likeness, (who is before) all likenesses; who is.. .

beginning, and ... to whom belong all ... within <him>. And all (lights) are in him, and all life is (in him), and (all) rest is <in him>, and (all) ... is in him, and ... and the Mother and the Son (are in him). This is the blessed one (alone). For All (pl.) have need of him, for because of him they all live. It is he who knows the All (pl.) ' within him, who contemplates the All (pl.) within himself. He is an incomprehensible one, but it is he who comprehends All (pl.) '. He receives them to himself. And nothing exists outside of him. But All (pl.) exist' within him. And he is boundary to them all, as he encloses them all, and they are all within him. It is he who is Father of the aeons, existing before them all. There is no place outside of him. There is nothing intelligible or anything at all, except the Only One. They look at his Incomprehensibility which is within them all, for he sets a boundary to them all. But they do not comprehend him, they marvel at his because he sets a boundary to them all. They strive ...

(lacuna of four lines)

Fragment of a Gnostic Hymn

Codex Brucianus.

Hear me as I sing praises to thee, O Mystery who existed
before every incomprehensible one and every endless one.
Hear me as I sing praise to thee, O Mystery, who hast shone
in thy mystery, so that the mystery which exists from the
beginning should be completed. And when thou didst
shine, thou didst become water of the ocean whose
imperishable name is this :

[AHZA]

Hear me as I sing praises to thee, O Mystery who existest
before every incomprehensible one and every endless one,
who hast shone in thy mystery. The earth in the middle of
the ocean was purified, of which the incomprehensible
name is this:

[AHZAE]

Hear me as I sing praises to thee, O Mystery who existest
before every incomprehensible one and every endless one,
who hast shone in thy mystery. All the powerful matter of
the ocean which is the sea, with every kind within it, was
purified, of which the incomprehensible name is this:

[AHZAHE]

Hear me as I sing praises to thee, O Mystery who existest
before every incomprehensible one and every endless one,
who hast shone in thy mystery. And as thou didst shine,

thou didst seal the sea and all things in it, because of the power within them rebelled, of which the incomprehensible name is this:

[.......]

Hear me as I sing praises to thee, O Mystery who existest before every incomprehensible one . . . .

Bruce Codex: Fragment of a Gnostic Text
"On the Passage of the Soul"

Archive Note:

This beautiful fragment tells the tale of the soul of the
Gnostic as it makes its passage out of creation, past the
"Archons of the Midst", toward its true home in the
Light. As the soul approaches each terrifying and fiercely
powerful Archon, it presents a key of liberation: to each is
given "the mystery of their fear", and the fear's
name. (These untranslatable Coptic names are only very
roughly represented in the text, below.) Knowing fear "face
to face", and naming it, the soul is liberated from the
Archons' restraint upon free passage.

On the Passage of the Soul
Through the Archons of the Midst

[Beginning missing] . . . the souls by theft:

when they take my soul to that place
it will give to them the mystery of their fear, which
is *XAPIHP*

And when they take it to the places of all the ranks of the
Paraplex,
the great and powerful Archon, who is spread out upon the
way of the Midst,
who carries off the souls by theft:

when they take my soul to that place
it will give to them the mystery of their fear, which
is *AXPW*

And again when they take my soul to the place of Typhon,
the great and powerful Archon with the face of an ass`s
who is spread out upon the way of the Midst,
who carries off the souls by theft:

> when they take my soul to that place
> it will give to them the mystery of their fear, which
is *PPAWP*

And again when they take my soul to the place of all the
ranks of Jachthanabas,
the great and powerful Archon,
who is full of anger, the successor of the Archon of the outer
darkness, the place in which all forms change,
who is powerful,
who is spread out upon the way of the Midst,
who carries off the souls by theft:

> when they take my soul to that place
> it will give to them the mystery of their fear which
is *AWHPNEUPSAZPA*

Printed in Great Britain
by Amazon